The Gymnastics Book

A Young Person's Guide to Gymnastics

The Gymnastics BOOK

Elfi Schlegel & Claire Ross Dunn

KEY PORTER BOOKS

Canadian Cataloguing in Publication Data

Schlegel, Elfi

The gymnastics book : a young person's guide to gymnastics

(Young athlete's series)

Includes Index.

ISBN 1-55263-284-9

1. Gymnastics – Juvenile literature. I. Dunn, Claire Ross. II. Title. III. Series.

GV461.S34 2000	j796.44	C00-931517-9

The publisher gratefully acknowledges the assistance of the Canada Council and the Ontario Arts Council. The publisher gratefully acknowledges the support of the Canada Council for the Arts and the Ontario Arts Council for its publishing program.

Key Porter Books Limited

70 The Esplanade

Toronto, Ontario

Canada M5E 1R2

www.keyporter.com

Design: Patricia Cavazzini

Printed and bound in Canada

00 01 02 03 6 5 4 3 2 1

Contents

Elfi Schlegel with gymnastic student, Sara Sowinski.

Preface

One Saturday in 1972, I wandered away from my arts and crafts class at the local recreation center and opened the doors to the gymnasium. Behind them I discovered what would become my playground for the next 15 years.

My first year was spent in a recreational gymnastics program—a one-hour, once-a-week affair that my mother observed from the back of the gym. A few years later, at age 10, I began to take gymnastics more seriously. I was named to the Ontario provincial team and competed in the Canadian National Championships. I finished 10th—a result that surprised many, including me—and I was described as the most promising gymnast in Canada. From then on I wanted to become an Olympian.

By watching Nadia Comaneci at the 1976 Montreal Olympics, I learned what it would take to make my dreams a reality. My teammates and I watched from the stands in awe while Nadia racked up all those perfect 10s. From that day on, if my coach asked me to practice a routine 10 times, I did so willingly.

In 1978, I was crowned Canadian National Champion, won 2 gold medals at the Commonwealth Games and became a member of the World Championship Team. A year later, Canada celebrated a monumental victory, winning gold over the United States at the Pan American Games in Puerto Rico. I was one step closer to my Olympic dream.

Then came disaster: the 1980 Olympic boycott. Although Canada decided to hold an Olympic Team tryout none the less (and I qualified), I remember thinking that it was a futile exercise. Most of my friends at the elite level were tired and disappointed. Some had even left the sport. I too considered quitting.

My father encouraged me to focus on a college scholarship instead. At the University of Florida, I became a six-time All-American and placed third in the 1985 NCAA Championship's individual all-around. Although I eventually left the sport on my own terms, I was able to savor my success.

Gymnastics has given me the opportunity to travel all over the world and make many new friends. It's also allowed me to turn gymnastics into a job, working as a commentator for CBC and CTV and now for NBC Sports. But perhaps most importantly, along with my sisters Chris and Andrea and my good friend Betty, it's given me the chance to open my own gymnastics club in Oakville, Ontario. Every day I teach what I've learned and, in turn, I learn new things from the budding gymnasts who participate in our programs.

So join me on a fun, exciting journey into the world of gymnastics. Let's learn together!

Elfi Schlegel

CHAPTER 1

Choosing Gymnastics

There are so many great reasons to choose gymnastics — and if you're reading this, you probably don't need much convincing.

Let's discuss some of the benefits that gymnastics has to offer.

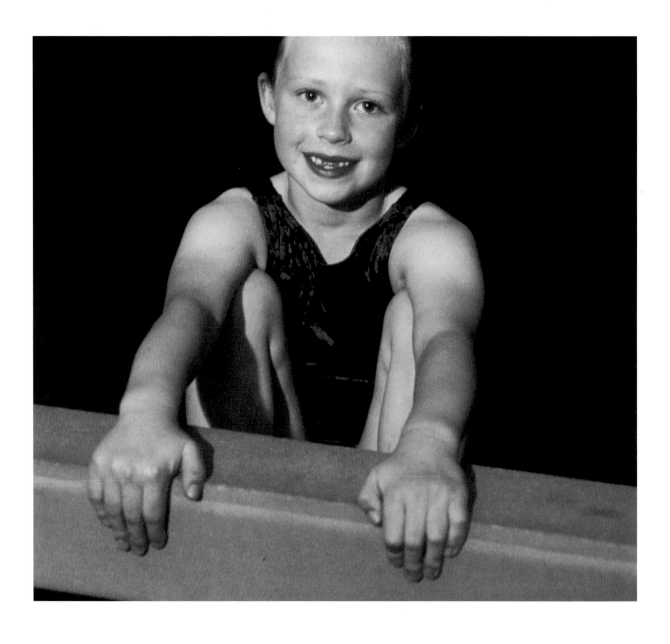

A Sport of All Sports

If you are involved in sports like diving and skating, your coach may encourage you to learn gymnastics to build your strength, flexibility, balance, coordination, agility and self-confidence.

But gymnastics doesn't just improve strength and flexibility — it also has positive effects on other aspects of your life.

A Sport for All Ages

People of all ages can benefit from gymnastics. Whether you are 2 years old attending Kindergym with a caregiver, or an adult learning gymnastics for the first time, gymnastics will help improve your flexibility and strength. It would be ideal to start learning gymnastics early in life, but it's never too late to start.

A Sport with No Gender Bias

One of the best things about gymnastics is that it's open to everyone. The apparatus doesn't discriminate — from rings to uneven bars, girls and boys are equally capable and welcome to try. At the Olympic level, however, only women compete on the balance beam and men compete on the pommel horse, though anyone can enjoy these events at a recreational level. Balance, coordination and strength are qualities that should be pursued by everyone.

And Speaking of the Apparatus …

Don't worry about having to leap over an Olympic-sized vault. Recreational facilities typically offer scaled-down, recreational-sized equipment. You can always progress to competition-sized apparatus later.

The Gymnastics Family

The gymnastics family has several branches: artistic and rhythmic gymnastics, trampoline and exciting new alternatives such as sport aerobics, sport acrobatics and tumbling. In artistic gymnastics various skills are performed on an apparatus. Women perform on the vault, uneven bars, balance beam and floor. Men perform on the floor, pommel horse, still rings, vault, parallel bars and horizontal bar. In rhythmic gymnastics skills are performed with an apparatus such as a rope, hoop, ball, ribbon and clubs. This book will focus on artistic gymnastics and trampoline, since they are typically what you'll encounter at the beginner recreational level. Once you've mastered these disciplines, however, you can explore other exciting options.

Overall …
the sport of gymnastics is all about fun, fitness and fundamentals:

FUN *because it's fun to jump, tumble and swing;*

FITNESS *because you'll gain flexibility, strength, power, muscular and cardiovascular endurance, balance, agility, coordination, body awareness and spatial orientation; and, above all,*

FUNDAMENTALS *because the moves you will learn — landings, static positions, locomotions, swings, rotations and springs — can be applied to almost any sport.*

CHAPTER 2

Knowing What to Look For

So. You've decided to start gymnastics. Now what?

Where do you go? What do you look for?

Your first step will be to discuss your goals with your parent or caregiver. Once you've identified what your goals are, looking for the right club and coach will be much easier.

Identifying Your Goals

What do you hope to learn, and how much time do you want to spend learning it? Do you want to be a recreational gymnast as well as explore other activities? Do you want to use gymnastics to become more flexible for skating or other sports? Do you want to be the next Nadia Comaneci, and redefine the sport of gymnastics?

If you're not sure of the answers just yet, don't worry; it may be too early to tell. The most important thing to know is whether you want to pursue a recreational or competitive program. Once you've figured that out, it will be easier to take the next step — choosing a club.

Choosing a Club

You have two options in terms of gymnastics facilities: public or private.

Public Facilities

Throughout most of North America, the YMCA and Parks and Recreation offer basic, recreational gymnastic programs. In the United States, Boys' and Girls' Clubs of America also offer various courses. Although the cost of public facilities is generally less than that of private clubs, staff members in public facilities usually do not have comparable qualifications to the staff who work in private facilities.

Private Facilities

Private gymnastics clubs focus solely on gymnastics. As a result, they typically offer a wider range of programs and specialize in coaching at both recreational and competitive levels. Most private facilities offer the following equipment:

• a carpeted floor exercise mat;
• a trampoline and mini-trampoline;
• a bar circuit that includes a circuit of rings, parallel bars, single bar and uneven bars, surrounded by safety mats;
• low-mounted balance beams (to help build confidence);
• a climbing rope with a bell on top;
• a height-adjustable vaulting apparatus;
• a special corner for Kindergym, with a jungle gym and mats; and
• plenty of creative circuits to keep you busy, learning and motivated.

Ask some of your friends who take gymnastics for recommendations on local clubs. Or contact the Gymnastics Federation (check the phone book) for local referrals. Then conduct your own research using the Internet (see page 118 for sites). The better informed you are, the better choice you'll make.

Signing Up

Once you've found a facility you like, you need certain information before signing up. First, find out about the facility's philosophy and program goals. Do they match yours? Most clubs provide a brochure that outlines their programs; if they don't, discuss the following issues with a member of their staff:

• Is the club covered by insurance, and will you have to also pay a personal liability insurance fee? These questions are crucial. If an injury occurs, the facility must be prepared to deal with it.
• Is the facility committed to teaching kids your age?
• What are the facility's safety policies and procedures? Are there regular safety and maintenance checks of the equipment?
• What's the cost of the program and how long does it last?
• Can you observe a class? If so, chat with the participants and find out about their experiences at the club.

• How long has the facility been in operation? Obviously, a club with an established reputation is ideal, but if it is new, ensure that the club has solid credentials.
• Is the building clean? After all, you want to feel comfortable running around in your bare feet.
• How large is the facility? Remember, bigger isn't always better. Smaller facilities cater directly to recreational athletes, and the equipment is specifically designed for recreational programs. Although some facilities offer competitive-specific equipment, you won't need it if you're only learning the fundamentals of the sport.

Choosing a Coach

It's also important to make inquiries about the coaching staff. After all, a great program starts with a great teacher.

• Does the coach have a gymnastics teaching certificate? In Canada, both recreational and competitive coaches must be certified by the National Coaching Certification Program (NCCP). Although certification is not mandatory in the United States, contact your local Gymnastics Federation for recommendations on clubs.

• Are the coaches trained in first aid?

• How many years of coaching experience does the coach have? In particular, ask about their experience coaching children. A coach must have the required skills or be supervised by a more experienced coach before leading a class by him- or herself.

Above all, you want coaches with great personality. The coach should be clear, positive, and enthusiastic, and have a sense of humor. After all, you're there to have fun! They should also help you feel comfortable, while teaching you new things and encouraging you to progress at your own pace.

Choosing a Program

Ask about the programs that are offered. Here's what to look for:

• What are the program's expectations? Is a certain level of experience required? Are programs available for your experience level?

• Can you join a class with your own age group? Usually, classes have a two- or three-year age range. You'll have more fun with the right age group, and the program will be tailored to you.

• How long is each class and how often does it take place? Think about your interests and your level of commitment, and choose a program accordingly.

• Are lesson plans available? All good programs have them. A lesson plan should be gauged to the ability of the class and be progression-oriented. Each step must be mastered before the next one can be tackled.

• What is the student–coach ratio? For children 5 years of age and older, the ratio should not exceed 10 to 1, although ideally it should be 8 to 1. For Kindergym (ages 2 to 5), the ratio should not exceed 6 to 1.

Registration

Find out when to register for the facility's programs. Usually, clubs will assign specific dates for registration. Don't miss this date — lots of fun awaits!

CHAPTER 3

Getting Started

So, you've found your club,
you've watched a class or two
and your first day is fast
approaching.

 What's next?

Elfi Schlegel at age 7, practicing the splits on the beam, during her first week at a recreational gymnastics club.

Safety

If you have long hair, tie it back so it doesn't get caught in the equipment. Do not wear jewelry to class for the same reason.

What to Wear

Unless your gymnastics club requires you to buy a uniform, you can probably make do with your own clothes. Loose cotton shorts and a T-shirt are just fine, as are footless leotards or tights, so you can feel the equipment with your bare feet. Shoes and slippers can slip and slide, so they aren't recommended.

Expectations

The first day can be very exciting, but it may also be overwhelming. Even if you're normally outgoing, you may feel shy on your first day. Here are some ways to ease your first-day jitters.

• Visit the facility in advance to get to know the program and staff.

• Choose your favorite T-shirt, shorts or gym suit, and set it out on a chair the night before class.

• Arrive on time. And remember, everyone starts as a beginner. Just have fun and be a good sport.

Elfi's Scrapbook

I remember the anticipation of my first gymnastics class. I talked about it all week. I'm sure my parents were relieved when the day finally arrived. My mother sat at the back of the gym, watching the first hour of a sport that would eventually consume 15 years of my life. Little did we know!

CHAPTER 4
The Healthy Gymnast

"Your body is your temple." "You are what you eat." We've all heard these sayings — and they're true. If you eat too much, your body won't perform. If you don't eat enough, your body won't have the fuel it needs to keep going. And if you eat junk food — well, enough said. Gymnastics is physically demanding, so it makes sense to eat properly and take care of your body.

Nutrition: Fueling the Machine

It is just as important for the once-a-week gymnast to practice good nutrition as it is for the competitive athlete pursuing the Olympic dream. Eating properly before a class will get you through 90 minutes of physical activity and assist you in sustaining your energy level for the entire session.

Remember to drink lots of water before and after class to prevent dehydration. This is especially true during the summer when you're sweating excessively from the heat.

Right before practice, eat a small snack instead of a full meal. Too much food will make you feel sluggish and tired. Fruit, vegetables, crackers and cheese, yogurt and juice are all good choices. Junk food is not. Junk food provides no nutritional value whatsoever. Instead, you will have an instant "sugar high" that won't sustain you for your class. Fueling your body properly helps you focus and maximize your workout.

Eating well will help you feel good and will enhance your performance.

Warming Up

Cardiovascular activity helps move blood to the muscles to warm them up and prepare them for work. Cardiovascular exercise will help you to work up a light sweat and increase your heart rate.

Before and after each 90-minute class, it's important to follow a regular three-step warm-up and cool-down routine like Walking to Running. Don't forget to periodically change your warm-up routine so you don't get bored!

Walking to Running

1. Begin by walking around the floor exercise mat.
2. Increase your speed to a slight jog. Now add some skipping, hopping or galloping in different directions for about 5 to 7 minutes.
3. Then move back to walking around the floor exercise mat. Remember to begin *and* end with walking so you ease in and out of the exercise.

Stretching

Now your body is prepared for stretching. This part of your routine lasts about 10 minutes. Begin with your neck and work your way down the rest of your body. Hold each stretch for a few seconds. Never bounce, and be careful to ease in and out of each move.

Neck

1. Slowly turn your head from side to side, looking at one wall and then the other. Do this 4 times on each side.

2. Tilt your head to bring your ear close to your shoulder. Leave your shoulder relaxed and down. Repeat 4 times on each side.

3. Drop your ear to your shoulder.

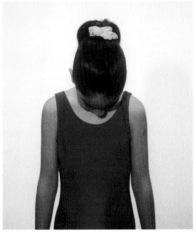

4. Roll your head forward, chin to chest. Continue rolling your head around until it reaches the opposite side. Repeat this head roll, holding each stretch position for at least 3 seconds.

Front angle.

Sides

With your legs shoulder-width apart, stretch one arm over your head, keeping it in line with your body. Allow the other arm to rest in front of your body. Bend over to the side until you can feel a stretch along your side. Your body should look like an arc when performing this stretch. Repeat twice on each side.

Side angle.

STRADDLE SIT

Sit comfortably on the floor with your legs apart. Keep your legs straight, knees facing the ceiling. Turn to one side and reach both arms along one leg, stretching toward your toes. Keep your chin up. Walk your arms in front of your body when switching sides. Repeat twice on each side, each time holding for 3 to 5 seconds.

Wrists

1. Clasp your hands together and roll your wrists around gently. This is sometimes referred to as "making milkshakes."

2. Now move your wrists in a roller-coaster motion.

3. Place your hands on the floor shoulder-width apart, facing your fingers away from your body. Lean forward gently to apply some weight on your wrists, then move back and repeat this action a couple of times.

4. Now turn your fingers in an outward direction to face your knees. Sit back on your heels to stretch your wrists. Release and repeat, holding for a few seconds.

Ankles

Sitting in a pike position (legs extended straight in front of you), cross one leg over the other, bending at the knee. Use one hand to hold your leg just above your ankle, with your other hand on your toes. Rotate your ankle in both directions slowly. Repeat with each ankle. Remember to sit up straight and maintain good body posture.

Hips

PSOAS STRETCH

The psoas is a hip flexor muscle. To do this stretch, kneel on one knee and place your other leg in front, bending at the knee. Place your hands on either side of your leg. Lean forward, but keep your chest and head up. Make sure your knee doesn't go over your toes. Hold this position for at least 30 seconds. If you don't feel much stretch, slowly move your foot out and away from your body. Repeat with each leg.

Legs

HAMSTRING STRETCH

You can do this stretch while you're performing the psoas stretch. From the psoas stretch position, push your body back so that your hips are directly over your supporting knee. Stretch out your front leg, keeping your hands on either side of your body. Hold the stretch for 30 seconds. To make this stretch more challenging, flex your front foot toward the ceiling.

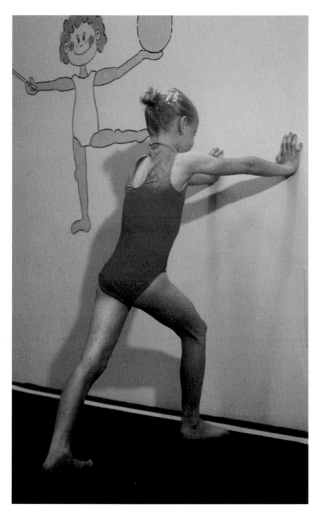

GASTROCNEMIUS STRETCH

This exercise will stretch out your calf muscles. Stand facing a wall. Place one leg in front of the other, your front leg slightly bent at the knee, your back leg straight. Point your toes toward the wall. Place your hands on the wall and, keeping your back heel on the floor, lean forward to feel the stretch in your calf. Hold this stretch for 30 seconds and then switch legs.

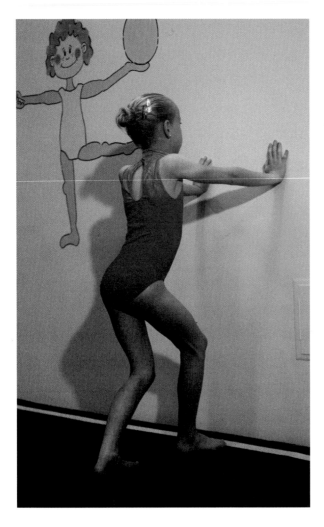

SOLEUS STRETCH

The soleus is another calf muscle, underneath the gastrocnemius and connected to the Achilles tendon. Position your body as you did for the gastrocnemius stretch, but this time bend your back knee into your front knee, keeping your back heel on the floor. You will feel this stretch much lower in the leg. Hold for at least 30 seconds, stretching as far as you feel comfortable.

Cooling Down

Cooling down is just as important as warming up. During your workout, your muscles will bulk up and produce lactic acid. Cooling down helps remove this buildup. First, participate in a fun cardiovascular activity for 5 to 7 minutes, like the ones we talked about on page 22. Then resume your stretching. All the warm-up stretches can also be used in the cool-down, so repeat some or all of them, depending on how much time you have. Most cool-downs last about 10 minutes. Remember: it's important to end with stretching to prevent stiffness the next day.

CHAPTER 5

Skills

"Skill" is the term used to define a single gymnastic movement that can be combined to create a routine of 2 or more elements. Every skill discussed in this chapter can be used as a basic gymnastic move that can then be adapted for more advanced moves; in other words, it will grow as you do. Just remember, photos and words can never do justice to the real thing. So it's important to practice at the gym.

In artistic gymnastics, skills are performed on an apparatus. Women perform on the vault, uneven bars, balance beam and floor. Men perform on the floor, pommel horse, still rings, vault, parallel bars and horizontal bar.

Elfi Schlegel at age 9, practicing her beam routine in her early years as a competitive gymnast.

Vault

When learning skills for the first time, a trapezoid-shaped vault made with multi-level blocks is ideal.

Hurdle

The hurdle is the approach and jump onto the spring board. Run toward the board, place one foot before the board, and jump with both feet on top of the board.

Hands
It's important to place your hands properly on top of the vault. Point your fingers forward, ensuring that your hands are flat on the vault, shoulder-width apart, and your shoulders are directly above your hands.

Landings

Landings are a fundamental dominant movement pattern of gymnastics. It's important to learn how to land on your feet properly, especially when you're jumping from different levels.

Jump From Vault

Jump off the vault with your arms forward for additional lift. Use your arms upon landing, placing them to the side and slightly forward for balance.

Land with your feet shoulder-width apart, heels on the floor (not springing back up). Bend your knees to absorb the shock.

Star

Tuck

Pike

Half turn

Here are some simple ways to jump off the vault: the star, tuck, pike and half turn.

Plyometric Jumps

Plyometric jumps are a series of rebounding jumps used to build explosiveness and power in the legs.

Rebounding Vault

Hurdle onto the board. Jump straight into the air, with your body extended and arms overhead. Land onto the first vault with your knees bent, arms down to your sides, and shoulders slightly in front of your feet. Rebound in the same straight jump position from the first vault to the second vault, absorbing the landing. Jump down to the safety mat, absorbing the landing again.

Courage Vault

The next progression is the courage vault. Jump from the board, place your hands onto the vault and tuck both knees up to your chest, placing them on top of the vault.

Squat on Vault

Jump off the board, place your hands shoulder-width apart on the vault, tuck your knees up to your chest and place your feet between your hands on top of the vault.

Straddle on Vault

Jump off the board, place your hands shoulder-width apart on the vault, straddle your legs and place your feet on either side of your hands with straight knees.

Tucked Front Vault

Jump off the board, turn your hands 90 degrees, lift your legs up to a tuck support position on both hands, and land on both feet in a standing position beside the vault. This vault can also be performed in a pike support position. (Pike means bending at the hips, with your legs stretched out in front.)

Pike support position.

Straddle over.

Straddle over landing.

Over the Vault

Once you feel comfortable performing these skills on the
vault, it's time to progress and
move over the vault.

Straddle Over

Jump off the board, place your
hands on the vault and straddle
your straight legs, lifting your
heels up and forward. You need
to be fairly flexible to clear the
vault. Your shoulders should be
slightly in front of your hands,
and your head should be face
forward. Use both hands to
push off the vault, and then
bring your feet together to
absorb the landing.

Variations include the squat
through, pike through and
front handspring.

Bars

A variety of bars can be used for recreational purposes: the single bar (or high bar), parallel bars, uneven bars and even the rings.

Strength Elements

It's important to practice strength moves to improve your overall gymnastic performance. You must be able to hold your body weight in order to progress. Here are some examples of strength elements.

Chin Up

With a straight body or knees in a tucked position, pull your body up to the single bar so that your chin is above the bar and not resting on top. Hold for 3 to 5 seconds. Rest and repeat.

Pull Up

Lying face up on an incline mat, hold on to the bar with your body in a stretched position. Beginning with your arms straight, maintain a straight body, and pull your upper body to the bar. It should look like you're performing an upside-down push-up.

Hold on to bar with body in stretched position.

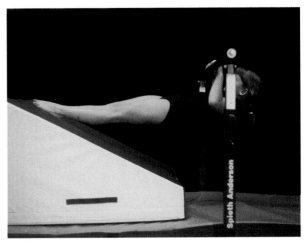

Pull upper body to the bar.

Tuck Hold

Working with a set of rings, and keeping them still, bend your elbows into your body and pull your entire body up to the rings. Tuck your knees into your chest and hold. A variation on this move is called an L-hold position, in which your legs are extended straight out from your body.

Tuck knees into chest and hold.

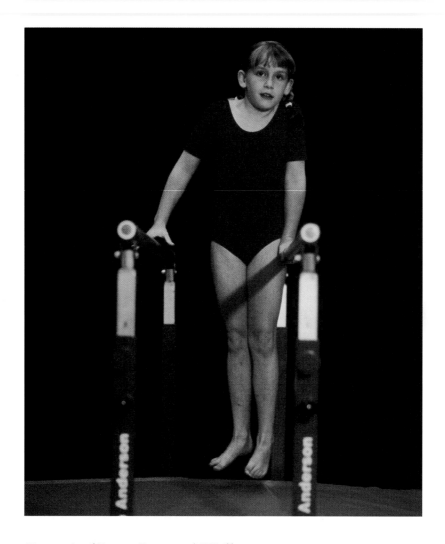

Penguin (Cross Support) Walks

This is an excellent way to build upper body strength. Working on the parallel bars, mount the end of the bars with your body in a vertical position, arms straight and close to your body. Begin walking along the length of the bars without allowing your feet to touch the ground.

Tuck hang.

Hangs

Hangs are static, or still, positions for which the shoulders are below the bar.

L hang.

Tuck Hang

Reach up to the bar (or rings), hold on with both hands, maintain straight arms and lift both your legs into a tuck position.

L Hang

Reach up to the bar (or rings) and extend your legs from the hips in an L position.

Star Hang
Stretch out your legs like a star.

Sole Hang
Hold on to the bar with straight arms, lift both legs up toward the bar and place your feet on the bar on either side of your hands. Keep your legs straight and your chin pulled in to your chest.

Front support: one of the most important positions on the bar.

Supports

A support is a static position that is performed with your shoulders above the bar.

Front Support

This is one of the most important positions on bars for beginning and ending elements. To move into position, jump up to the bar, with your body and arms straight. Push downward through your arms to raise your body, with your shoulders slightly in front of your hands. Ensure that the bar rests across your hips, not your stomach.

Hang position.

Swings

Swings are an integral part of gymnastics on the bars. To swing safely, you must have a good understanding of hangs and supports.

Banana position.

Beat Swing

Begin in a hang position from the bar. Gently hollow your body, with your feet slightly in front. This is known as the "banana position." Then reverse the position with your feet moving behind, creating a back banana position. Continue moving back and forth, from front banana to back banana. Re-grasp (let go and grab the bar again) in the hollow position at the top of the back swing to readjust and hold on.

Back banana position.

Glide Swing

You can learn this swing by starting on an incline mat. Hold on to the bar, with your body slightly bent at the hips. Lift both feet off the ground. Your body will be in a stretched position at the middle of the swing. Swing back to your start position, keeping your feet in front of your body.

1. Hang position.

Long Swing

This is one of the most basic and important swings. Extend your body forward in a hollow position with your feet in front. As you swing back, your feet will remain in the same position. You will have to re-grasp the bar on the top of the back swing. Keep the height of the swing (called the amplitude) low in order to develop your skill at re-grasping the bar. As you increase your strength and improve your technique, you will increase your amplitude. Remember to focus on control before height.

2. Hollow position with feet in front.

3. Swing back.

Rotations

Rotation is the movement of your body around itself or an apparatus.

Forward Roll Down

From a front support position on the bar, begin to lean your body forward by tucking your chin into your chest and bending at your waist. Rotate slowly around the bar, keeping your body in a tucked position. Continue the forward roll action around the bar until you end in a standing position on the floor.

1. Front support position.

2. Slowly rotate around bar.

3. End in standing position.

Hip Pullover

Holding on to the bar, perform a chin-up, kicking your legs up and over, bending at your hips to sandwich the bar between your upper and lower body. Continue the circle, allowing your hands to slide around the bar, and finish in a front support position.

2. Kick legs up and over, bending at the hips.

1. Chin-up.

3. Continue to circle around bar.

4. Finish in front support position.

Backward Hip Circle

From a front support position, lean slightly forward with your shoulders, bending in with your hips. Push your hips away from the bar with straight arms, maintaining a hollow body. Your hips should return to the bar like a magnet to complete the full 360-degree rotation. As your body rotates backward, tuck your chin into your chest. Your hands should move freely around the bar. End in a front support.

1. Front support position.

2. Lean slightly forward, push hips away from bar.

3. Rotate backward.

4. End in front support.

Balance Beam

In a recreational setting, it is best to use a low balance beam when starting out. This helps gymnasts gain confidence while learning new skills.

Mounts and Dismounts

Mounts and dismounts are ways of getting on and off the apparatus.

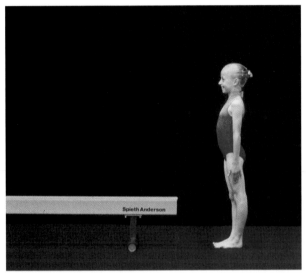

1. Stand facing end of beam.

2. Use both feet to jump onto beam.

Jump to Squat

Stand facing the end of the beam. Use both feet to jump onto the beam, with one foot slightly in front of the other, landing in a bent knee position. Use your arms to maintain balance, while keeping your head neutral and your eyes focused on the end of the beam.

Straddle Mount

Stand facing the side of the beam. Place your hands on the beam, shoulder-width apart, and jump onto the beam, straddling your straight legs, with your shoulders slightly in front of your hands.

1. Place hands on beam, shoulder-width apart.

2. Jump onto beam, straddling with straight legs.

1. Bring one leg up in a tucked position.

Wolf Mount

Stand facing the side of the beam. Place your hands on top of the beam and jump up, bringing one leg up in a tucked position and placing that foot on the beam, between your hands. Bring your other leg up on top of the beam, outside your hands, and extend it. Try to do these two moves simultaneously. Your arms can remain on top of the beam or you can extend them outward.

2. Bring other leg up on top of beam and extend.

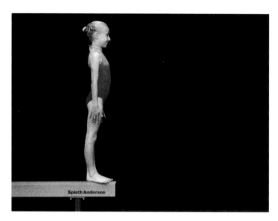

1. Stand on beam.

Tuck Jump Dismount

Stand on the beam. Jump to a tuck position in the air from the end or side of the beam, lifting your arms over your head. At the top of the jump, place your hands on top of your knees before landing on two feet, with your arms to the side. Bend your knees to absorb the landing.

2. Tuck position in air, hands on top of knees.

3. Land with bent knees to absorb landing.

1. Star jump.

Star Jump Dismount

Stand on the beam. Jump up in the air, straddling your legs to the side, and bring your legs back together, absorbing the landing on the mat.

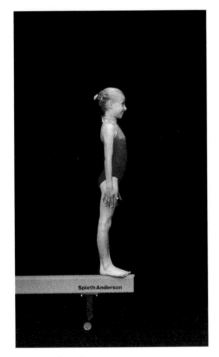

1. Stand on beam.

2. Jump half turn in air.

Jump Dismounts with Rotations

Stand on the beam. Jump off and make a half turn, with your arms in the air and with a straight body, absorbing the landing on the mat. You can eventually progress to full turns and greater.

57

1. Walk forward along beam, one foot in front of the other.

Walking

Begin by walking forward, backward and sideward on the beam. Then progress to walking on your toes.

Walk Forward

Walk forward along the beam by slightly turning out your feet, one foot in front of the other. Focus on the end of the beam, and stretch your arms to the side for balance. (It's useful to imagine your arms as the long pole used for balance by a circus tight-rope walker.)

2. Focus on end of beam, stretch arms to side.

1. Feel the side of the beam as you place your foot behind.

2. Keep your arms to the sides and head neutral.

Walk Backward

Walk backwards by placing one foot behind the other. Again, focus on the end of the beam. Feel the side of the beam as you place your foot behind, keeping your arms to your sides and your head neutral.

Walk Sideward

Facing the side of the beam, step one foot to the side and close the other foot to it. Continue moving in the same direction until you've reached the end of the beam. Keep your head neutral and focus on the beam mats in front of you.

1. Right foot in front.

Grapevine Walk

Place one foot in front of the other (or behind) and continue the motion sideward down the beam.

2. Right foot steps behind.

"Dip" Walk
(Forward and Backward)

Walk forward by bending one knee slightly and "dipping" the other foot down along the side of the beam. Then bring that same foot up on top of the beam in front of the support foot. Reverse the process when walking backwards.

1. Bend one knee slightly and "dip" the other foot down.

2. Reverse the process when walking backwards.

Lunge Step

Step forward on one foot, bending your knee while your back knee rests on the beam. Your front knee will be directly over your front foot, with your arms stretched out to the side. Stand up and step forward with the back foot, repeating the lunge, arms to the side.

Statics

Statics are "held" or "still" positions. Many statics require good balance.

Stork Stand

Stand on the beam, arms stretched out to the side for balance. Raise one foot up to the knee of your support leg by bending at the knee of your working leg. Hold this position for a few seconds. Switch legs.

Front Scale

From a standing position, lift
one leg behind you. Lower your
upper body as your leg lifts in
the air. Keep both legs straight,
arms to the side for balance,
and keep your head neutral.

Knee Scale

From a lunge step position (see page 63), move your front leg behind and up, leg extended, placing your hands in front and on the beam for support.

V Sit

While sitting on the beam,
place your hands on the beam,
behind your hips, and raise
your legs in front of your body
into a V position.

Leaps

Leaps are one of the elements found in the dominant movement pattern of springs.

Hitch Kick Leap

Standing on the beam, raise one leg into the air, bringing the other leg up to it. Touch them together and land back on the take-off foot.

1. Raise one leg into the air.

2. Bring the other leg up.

3. Land on take-off foot.

Jumps

Stretched Jump

Stand with one foot in front of the other. Push off of both feet and stretch your body in the air, with your arms extending up.

Land with both feet on the beam. This is a fairly basic jump and can be performed in various positions: star, tuck, pike, straddle and turning jumps, including rotations of 90, 180 and 360 degrees.

1. Stand with one foot in front.

2. Push off, arms extended.

3. Landing.

Star.

Tuck.

Pike.

1. *Rise up onto the balls of the feet.*

Turns

Pivot Turn

Stand on the beam, facing the end with one foot in front of the other. Rise up onto the balls of your feet and turn 180 degrees toward your back foot to face the other end of the beam.

2. *Turn 180 degrees.*

3. *End facing the other end of the beam.*

1. Squat position.

2. Turn 180 degrees.

Squat Turn

Stand on the beam facing the end. Lower your body to a squat position. Turn 180 degrees toward the back foot to face the other end of the beam. It is easier to perform this skill while on your toes, with your arms stretched out to the side for balance.

3. End facing the other end of the beam.

1. Lift one leg in front.

Forward Kick Turn

Lift one leg in front and perform a half turn on the other foot. Finish with your leg up behind your body, keeping your arms to the side for balance.

2. Turn, finishing with leg behind body.

Floor Exercise

Recreational skills can be taught with the aid of an incline mat as well as blocks. Eventually, you can progress to the floor. Here are a few common floor skills and the progressions involved.

Rolls

Log Rolls

You will need to learn this basic roll before progressing to forward and backward rolls. This move will help to determine whether you can maintain a straight and tight body position. The log roll can be performed on an incline mat, level floor mat or wedge mat.

Begin by laying down on the wedge mat, with your body straight and fully extended, your arms over your head. Roll your entire body, like a pencil, and continue rolling on the floor or wedge, maintaining a tight body position. Repeat this move, rolling up the wedge to increase the difficulty. You can also do a sideward variation by tucking your knees into your chest.

1. Stand on the high end of the wedge.

2. Tuck chin into chest and push off to roll over.

3. Finish in a straight stand.

Forward Roll

Let's continue using the wedge for our introduction to rolls. When you're comfortable with your progress, you can perform the rolls directly on the floor, with many variations, including different starting and finishing positions.

Tucked Forward Roll

Stand on the high end of the wedge. Squat down, bending at your knees and hips and place your hands flat, shoulder-width apart, in front of your feet. Raise your hips and tuck your chin into your chest. Push off your feet, roll over and finish in a straight stand.

1. Standing with feet in straddle position.

Straddle Forward Roll

Stand with your feet in a straddle position. Reach your hands between your legs on the mat and perform a forward roll, tucking your chin to your chest. Push off your hands and stand in a straddle to finish. These rolls can also be performed in a pike position.

2. Reach hands between legs and perform forward roll.

3. Push off hands and stand in straddle to finish.

Rock 'N' Roll

Sit in a tuck position and roll backward and forward like a ball. Your head doesn't touch the floor.

Rock 'n' Roll.

1. Tuck position.

2. Tuck knees and chin in, with arms over head.

3. Roll backward, and up to start position.

Rock 'N' Roll Part II

Sitting in a tuck position on the floor or the wedge, hold your arms over your head, as if you were holding a large beach ball. Place your hands over one another, with your palms facing out. Tuck your chin into your chest and roll backward, but not over. Allow your arms to hit the mat first, protecting your head as you roll. Roll back up to the start position. Practice this move several times.

1. Squat position.

2. Roll backwards.

3. Let arms help to push over, into a stand.

Backward Roll

Now that you have tried these two progressions, you can try the backward roll.

Sit in a squat position on the high end of the wedge, facing away from the down slope. Using the same beach ball arm position, roll backwards, keeping your knees and chin into your chest. Let your arms hit the mat first to protect your head. They'll also help push you all the way over, followed by the rest of your body. Finish in a stand.

Handstand

The handstand is a key gymnastics skill. You'll see it time and time again on most apparatus. Try to master these progressions before attempting a handstand.

Front Support Walk (Push-up Position)

Assume a front support position on the floor, as if you were going to do push-ups. Now raise your feet on a block. Proceed to walk your hands along the floor, as your feet follow on the block, maintaining a strong front support position. Practice this a few times, keeping your stomach muscles tight and body stretched. Once you've accomplished this, you are ready to move on.

1. Raise feet on block in front support position.

2. Take small steps to the side with hands and feet.

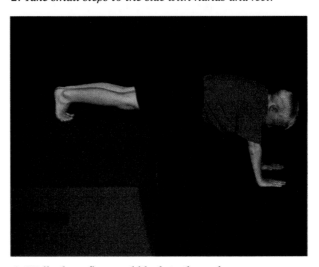

3. Walk along floor and block to the end.

Walk Up the Wall

Place a mat against a wall. In a front support position, walk your feet up the wall, as far as you are comfortable. Maintain a tight body position, avoiding an arch in the lower back. While your feet are moving, walk your hands closer toward the wall. Hold this position comfortably. Don't fall out of the handstand position. Maintain your strength as you walk down.

1. Front support position.

2. Walk feet up the wall.

3. Finish in handstand position.

Cartwheel to Handstand on Wall

Keep the mat against the wall. Standing with your side to the wall, place your hands on the floor, turning them 90 degrees from your body, shoulder-width apart. Kick one leg up to the wall, following quickly with the other leg. Your body should be stretched and tight. Hold for balance. Come down slowly the same way you went up.

1. Stand with side to the wall.

2. Kick up to handstand position.

3. Lower legs back to start position.

1. Face the wall.

2. Kick to handstand position.

Kick to Handstand

Face the wall. It will not act as your support, but as a safety measure. Place your hands in front of your feet, shoulder width apart. Kick one leg to a handstand, the other leg following quickly. Keep your body stretched, avoiding a banana position. Keep your head neutral, hands on the ground and your eyes looking at the floor. Hold this position for strength and balance, then step slowly down to the floor. When you are comfortable with this progression, move away from the wall completely. Your coach will stand nearby to shadow.

Cartwheels

This is one of the most popular basic moves in gymnastics.

1. Straddle stand position.

2. Place one hand on the rope.

Hand-Hand-Foot-Foot

First, let's look at the basic elements of a cartwheel. Place a rope in a circle on the floor. In a straddle stand position, face the inside of the circle. Moving to the side, place one hand on the rope, followed by the other hand. Kick your leg around, followed closely by the other leg to swivel around the rope.

3. Kick leg around.

4. Finish position.

1. Starting position.

2. Place hands on block and kick up.

3. Kick over the block.

4. Land with the opposite foot.

Cartwheel over Block

Now move to an elevated block. Place one foot in front of the other on the floor. Place your hands on the block, turning them 90 degrees from your body. In a cartwheel action, kick over the block to the other side, landing with your opposite foot. Repeat this movement on either side of the block.

Cartwheel on the Floor

Now try your full cartwheel on the floor, passing through the handstand position and finishing in a lunge (with one slightly bent leg in front of the back straight leg).

2. Kick over through handstand position.

1. Starting position.

3. Follow through to landing.

4. Lunge position.

Trampoline

The trampoline is a tremendous form of exercise — not to mention a lot of fun! Everyone loves the feeling of jumping on the trampoline and being suspended in the air — it's like being on a roller coaster.

Safety

Before starting, your coach will point out a few basic safety measures that must be respected.

• Only one person may use the trampoline at any time. Two people poses a risk of injury.
• The center is the safest place to jump on the trampoline.
• Hold your head neutral, eyes slightly down, focusing on the end of the trampoline.
• The safest way to land is with your weight equally distributed on both legs as they come into contact with the trampoline.
• It's important to know when to stop — also known as "putting on the brakes." Injuries can occur if you're jumping out of control. If this happens, put on the brakes.

1. Jump into the air.

Foot-to-Foot Skills

Straight Jump

Stand still on the trampoline, without bouncing. Jump into the air, extending your arms up and forward, keeping your body in a straight line. Land on both feet, relaxing your knees. Now repeat with a low bounce.

2. Land on both feet.

Tuck Jump

Follow the same instructions for the straight jump, but at the highest point of the jump, bring your knees up to your chest in a tuck position, with your hands touching the tops of your knees. Straighten your body before landing on the trampoline.

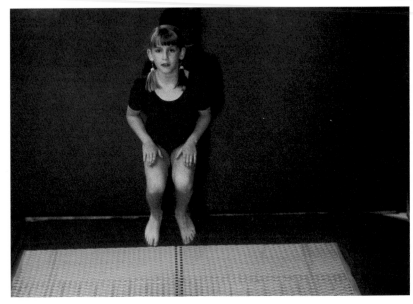

Bring knees up to chest in tuck position.

Pike Jump

Jump up, bringing your legs up in front and extending them from the hips. Reach your arms forward, and touch the top of your feet with your fingers. Do not lean too far forward and keep your head neutral.

Jump up with legs extended in front.

Star Jump

Follow the same instructions for a straight jump, but this time, extend your legs and arms out in a star position at the highest point of the jump.

Extend legs and arms in star position.

Twisting Jumps

The takeoff for twisting jumps is similar to straight jumps. Lift your body off the trampoline, with your arms in the air. But this time, twist your shoulders and hips. To keep your balance, look straight ahead both before and after the twist. Start by doing a simple half-twist jump with no bounce. Add more bounce once you're comfortable. When you've mastered the half twist, you can progress to a full twist.

1. Twist shoulders and hips.   *2. Landing.*

Seat Drop

Jump up, lifting your legs and extending them forward. Land in an L sitting position on the trampoline, with your hands on the trampoline, fingers pointing forward. Begin this skill with no bounce and eventually progress to a low bounce.

Land in an L sitting position.

Hand-and-Knee Drop

Squat down low to the trampoline, leaning your body forward. Jump down to your hands and knees, letting them land simultaneously on the trampoline. Keep your arms relaxed when hitting the trampoline bed. Your back should be level, with your head looking at a focal point at the end of the trampoline. When you are comfortable, eliminate the squat start and begin from a standing position.

1. Squat, leaning forward.

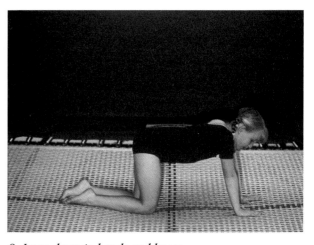

2. Jump down to hands and knees.

Front Drop

Start from the hand-and-knee drop position on the trampoline. With no bounce, extend your body and land in a front drop position. Your body should be completely stretched with your arms bent to your sides. Hold your head high enough to be able to see the end of the trampoline. When you become confident, begin from a standing position.

1. Hand-and-knee drop position.

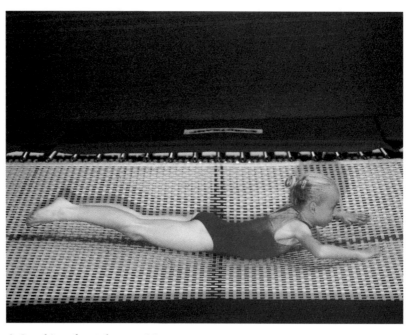

2. Land in a front drop position.

1. Start in a low squat position.

Back Drop

From a low squat position, do a very small jump backwards from both feet. You should land flat onto your back, without your legs or head touching the trampoline. Your head and your arms are up toward the ceiling.

2. Land flat on back.

Combinations

Once you've mastered these skills, you can perform them in combination. For example, you could perform:

• a seat drop to a hand-and-knee drop, or vice versa,

• a tuck jump to a star jump to a straight jump,

• a seat drop to front drop.

The possibilities for mini-routines are endless. Practice often, be safe and have fun!

CHAPTER 6

Competition: Raising the Bar

No doubt you're loving your recreational gymnastics class. Now you want to take the sport to the next level — competitive gymnastics.

Lots of challenges — and exciting times — lie ahead. Here's an overview of the competitive gymnastics world and some things to consider when deciding whether you want to join it.

Elfi Schlegel at age 18 competing at The University of Florida's NCAA championships.

A Look at the Greats in Gymnastics

When gymnastics first became popular, athletes were often old enough to be married. But in recent years, gymnastics has been coined the "Cinderella sport" because female gymnasts are often the youngest athletes in competition. Audiences around the world marvel at how focused, motivated and disciplined these athletes are for their age. And with every new Olympics, a young gymnast manages to steal the limelight and become internationally known by her first name only. She is a star who transcends both borders and languages.

These are just a few of the gymnasts who have made a difference and pushed the boundaries of gymnastics.

Elfi's Scrapbook

OLGA KORBUT

The first time I ever watched gymnastics on television, it was the 1972 Olympics held in Munich, Germany. The star of the games was 17-year-old Olga Korbut, the youngest member of the Soviet Union gymnastic team. She performed moves that had never been seen before, and performed incredible acrobatic skills on the uneven bars, including a back flip from the high bar to the low bar. She was also the first athlete ever to perform a back somersault on the balance beam. I was in awe!

The Russians, always so stoic and disciplined, were real leaders in the sport of gymnastics. But the world fell in love with Olga because she revealed her human side: she laughed with the audience, played to them throughout her floor routine and cried when she fell off the apparatus. Even though she didn't win, people were drawn to her — she was an athlete with heart.

Olga Korbut competing on the beam at the 1972 Munich Olympics.

Nadia Comaneci receiving a gold medal at the 1976 Montréal Olympics.

Elfi's Scrapbook

NADIA COMANECI

At the 1976 Olympics in Montreal, I was a new addition to the Canadian National Team, but too young to compete. I watched from the sidelines as Romania's Nadia Comaneci performed. Every night I returned to see if I could spot a difference in her routines, but I couldn't. She was perfect. The scoreboard couldn't accommodate a perfect 10 — so her score came up as 1.0. Even the announcers weren't sure how to read her score! Nadia scored 7 perfect 10s. She was so popular she quickly became a household name and helped put her country on the map. No gymnast has ever come close to Nadia's achievements.

Elfi's Scrapbook

MARY LOU RETTON
At the 1984 Olympics in Los Angeles, California, Mary Lou Retton became the first American gymnast to win an Olympic gold medal. Her coach was Bela Karolyi, the same coach who made Nadia Comaneci a champion. Although Mary Lou wasn't the favorite to win, she thrived on pressure. She had incredible strength and determination. Her bubbly, infectious personality made people marvel at her seemingly boundless energy. Winning the gold made her an instant celebrity; she did commercials, made "celebrity" appearances and even ended up on a Wheaties cereal box!

Mary Lou Retton getting a hug from coach Bela Karolyi after winning the gold at the 1984 Los Angeles Olympics.

Vitaly Scherbo receiving a gold medal at the 1992 Barcelona Olympics.

Elfi's Scrapbook

VITALY SCHERBO

In Barcelona in 1992, Belorussian Vitaly Scherbo became the first male gymnast to win 6 gold medals. He won more medals than any athlete at that Olympics — in fact, more than any gymnast in a single Olympics.

Making the Transition from Recreation to Competition

The decision to progress to competitive gymnastics involves 3 parties: you, your parents and your coach. You are probably ready to proceed if you have mastered the skills taught in your recreational gymnastics class; if you grasp new skills quickly and understand the progressions in each move; and if you show consistency in your work. Most importantly, though, you must be mentally ready: you have to love gymnastics! If you aren't, the long hours of training and the rigorous demands of competing simply won't be worth the sacrifice.

From a coach's perspective, you're ready to compete when you've proven you're easily "coachable": you have confidence, team spirit, a drive to excel and a willingness to improve.

Some recreational clubs operate a small competitive program within their facility. These programs encourage students to develop simple routines that are shown only to parents and other club members. Even though there are no official judges, the students have the opportunity to "perform" for an audience, which can be a good indicator of whether they are ready to compete.

Elfi Schlegel at age 9, practicing her beam routine in her home gym.

Elfi Schlegel: The Life of a Competitive Gymnast

Time and Commitment

It's hard to believe how quickly competing took over my life. I went from training one hour a week, to 2 days a week for 3 hours a session, to 5 days a week for a total of 15 hours. And I was only 10 years old. Two years later, my hours doubled. By the time I was 14, I was away from home for 2 months of the year and even missed my prom. Certainly, that lifestyle is not for everybody, but for me, it was a question of devotion. I was in love with gymnastics. Many athletes train at least 5 hours at a time, 6 days a week. That's 30 hours a week at the gym. On top of that, traveling to competitions around the world can consume another 2 months a year. This kind of commitment deeply affects other areas of your life, so think carefully about the consequences before you decide to become a competitive gymnast.

If you're still interested, here are some things to watch out for, some ways to cope with what can be a very demanding schedule and a bit about the exciting world that awaits you.

School

Gymnastics may feel like a world of its own, but getting a good education is also vital. You need to find a way to excel at both school and gymnastics. So, approach your teachers and discuss your gymnastics schedule. They will have to provide you with homework to cover missed classes, grant extended homework deadlines and postpone tests. Whenever I traveled, I would take my books and assignments with me. Then while I was away, I would take notes about my travels. When I returned, I would make class presentations about the countries I'd visited. I became a real pro at geography!

Family

I could never have embraced the world of competitive gymnastics without my family's support. Avoid potential conflict by being an active participant in your family's life. Do your share of the chores. Attend your siblings' extra-curricular activities.

Although my older sister, Chris, also competed in gymnastics, there was never any rivalry between us. In fact, once, when I was competing on the floor, my sister was so involved in my performance she didn't hear her own name being called for the beam! Early on in her career she decided to become a coach and began training when she turned 16. Soon she became my coach away from the gym. She offered me valuable insight into my performance on the road. My younger sister, Andrea, also grew to love (and compete in) gymnastics. We would make up routines in our bedrooms and teach each other cool gymnastic tricks. My brother, Peter, loved hockey. Sports was something that held our family together.

Clockwise from left to right: Chris, Elfi, Peter, and Andrea Schlegel.

Elfi Schlegel chats with international gymnasts at a 1978 competition in Shanghai, China.

Financial Costs

When I decided to compete, my parents had to pay a lot of fees — club fees, new suits for competition, gas for driving to and from the gym. When I made the National Team, the Canadian government paid me a stipend every month to cover costs. Then, after I won a World Cup medal for Canada, the stipend doubled. It wasn't a lot — but it made me feel official, and eased some of the financial burden from my family. If your family doesn't have a car, see if you can car-pool to the club with other kids from class. Sharing driving and gas will be a relief for your parents, and you'll have a chance to socialize with fellow gymnasts.

Friends

Instead of thinking that competing would take me away from my friends, I chose to take a different perspective. Competing gave me the chance to make new friends, both at the gym and around the world. Meeting new people and learning about new places became my favorite part of traveling. And I still keep in touch with some of the people I met during that time.

But the truth is, having an exciting lifestyle can often be difficult on friends at home. They may feel left out — or left behind. Even if I sometimes felt far away from my school friends, I would try not to let distance get in the way. Focus on what you share, not what divides you. Don't forget to ask your friends about their lives. Celebrate their victories and be humble about yours.

Physical Therapy and Injuries

Increased training time often means sore muscles and therefore physical therapy. This is where you, your coach and a physical therapist make every effort to keep your body injury-free, and prevent any injuries from becoming chronic.

To minimize the need for physical therapy, you can do the following: always warm up and cool down properly, and use ice or heat on your muscles, where appropriate.

Coaches

The world of competitive gymnastics involves many people. Your personal coach may become a friend, a parent figure, even a role model. Competitive coaches want to maximize your talent and help you achieve new goals. This relationship may have ups and downs, especially considering how much time you will spend together. Be prepared for both good days and bad days. Sometimes you may not feel like training, but a good coach will have the ability to motivate you anyway.

Sports Psychologists

National team athletes work with sports psychologists on a regular basis. They help you focus on your training through mental imagery — reviewing your routines the night before a competition, practicing breathing techniques and learning how to calm your nerves. Eventually this becomes a regular part of your routine and almost as important as the physical training itself.

Judges

Competitive gymnasts receive an enormous amount of critical feedback, from coaches, judges and other athletes. Dealing with a judged sport is not always easy. Regardless of your score, remember that you tried your best.

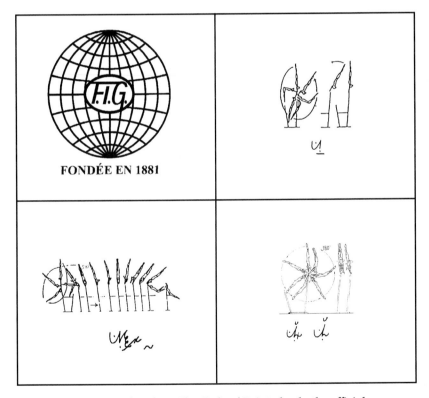

These images were taken from The Code of Points *book, the official gymnastics symbol guide.*

𝒟id 𝒴ou 𝒦now...

Judges use a form of shorthand made up of over 1000 symbols to quickly notate different elements of a gymnast's routine. The symbols are listed in a book called The Code of Points.

A Day in the Life of a Female Competitive Gymnast

KIM ZMESKAL-BURDETTE

The first day I walked into a gym, I was holding my babysitter's hand. Her daughter was taking classes at the gym that later become Karolyi's Gymnastics. I remember peering through the balcony railings, planning how I would convince my mother to let me take gymnastics too.

The day of my first competition, I woke up as early as if it were Christmas morning. I was excited — and nervous! I took hours to get ready. I danced through my routines in the living room. But no matter what I did, I grew more nervous the closer we got to the gym. Those nerves lasted right through my bar and beam routines. By the time I got to the vault and floor — my best events — I felt right at home. I learned to like those butterflies. I could feel they'd be my friends for years to come.

Who knew that first competition experience would lead to winning the World Gold Medal in 1991? I have never been more honored than when I stood on top of that awards podium, my right hand over my heart, listening to the American anthem. Thousands of people cheered. I stepped off the podium in a daze and my teammate, Hilary Grivich, cheered, "You won! You are the World Champion!" I could hardly believe it.

Kim Zmeskal-Burdette
1991 American World Champion
1992 Olympian, Bronze Team, USA

How to Get Competitive

In the United States, the Women's Junior Olympic Program is divided into 4 major sections. The first section's Levels 1 through 4 are non-competitive, developmental levels. Levels 2, 3 and 4 may also be used as a recreational competitive program. The second section, Levels 5 and 6, is compulsory. The third section, Level 7, bridges the gap between compulsory and optional exercises. Competitive opportunities are provided up to and including the USA Gymnastics State Championships. The fourth section encompasses optional Levels 8, 9 and 10. Additional competitive opportunities are provided at these levels, with the Level 10 season culminating at the Junior Olympic National Championships.

Although there is no recognized "Junior Olympic Program" in Canada, there is a provincial and national system with various levels. The first level is the Pre-Novice level, followed by Novice, Pre-Junior, Junior, High-Performance Junior, Senior and High-Performance Senior. Within these levels, there may be as many as 3 categories divided by age (these levels vary from one province to another).

If you have any questions about how these competitive streams are organized in your area, ask your coach or contact your regional Gymnastics Federation (see page 118 for contact information).

Competitive Training Schedule

At the senior Olympic level, many athletes will train 6 times a week, twice a day, anywhere from 35 to 40 hours a week. A lot of athletes keep a log book to record their progress during training. I did. Although every athlete's schedule will be different, on the next page is a sample of what a day in the life of an Olympic or National Team athlete might look like.

Competitive Training Schedule

Life as a gymnast can be pretty demanding. Here's an average competitive training schedule for just another average day.

7:00 am	Wake up, have a good breakfast
7:30 am	Leave for morning practice
8:00 am	Arrive at gym
8:10-8:30 am	Warm-up
8:30-9:00 am	Perform conditioning exercises and strength training workouts

Today: chin-ups, pull-ups, rope climbing, running drills, cardio endurance (jump rope and stationary bike)

9:00-9:30 am	Perform specific drill exercises on 2 apparatus
	Beam: work on turns for better balance. Floor: went through choreography
9:30-10:00 am	Stretch and cool-down
10:15 am	Travel home/eat snack in car (fruit)
10:45-11:30	Nap
11:30 am	Lunch
12:00 pm	Homework, tutor, physical therapy **Notes:** ice ankles
1:30 pm	Leave for afternoon gym workout (continue homework in car)
2:00-2:30 pm	Warm-up for more rigorous workout **Notes:** taped ankles
2:30-3:00 pm	Vault workout

Goal: Yurchenko double twist

– 3 sprints down the runway to warm-up

– 5 simple warm-up vaults in the foam pit

– practice Yurchenko double twist x 10

Notes: got better lift off the horse. Coach said the Yurchenko twist was looking cleaner but could still improve on round-off back handspring to get more bump off horse. We're almost there. Need to work on landing.

3:00-3:45 pm	Bar workout. Goal: more consistency on the Tkatchev release
	– warm-up with glide kips and handstands

       – warm-up important combinations and 2 dismounts

       – practice 7 bar routines

Notes: good flow with 4 routines; had problems with last 3 because of Tkatchev. Still need to work on getting more height in this move. Coach said handstand positions throughout bar routine were improved from yesterday. Stuck the landings on the dismounts.

3:45-4:45 pm   Beam workout. Goal: adding the flip-flop tuck full

       – warm-up with walking, jumps and dance combinations

       – warm-up skills like flip flop, layout combination, flip-flop full and dismount

       – practice 10 beam routines

Notes: excited about adding my difficult flip flop full. Hit 5 out of 10. Need to improve on consistency.
       Other skills in routine solid, still need to get rid of small hop on landing.

4:45-5:30 pm   Floor workout. Goal: make it through to 3rd tumbling pass

       – warm-up with easy tumbling runs

       – practice tumbling passes from routine—double Arabian and double layout punch front pass

       – dance combinations

       – practice 3 routines and review choreography

Notes: energy better today. No problem completing triple twist at end of routine. Finally! Put my hands down on the double Arabian in the first routine, but corrected the mistake for the next 2.
Double layout punch front was awesome. Still need to work on triple turn to Schushanova combination.

5:30-6:00 pm   Cool-down

Notes: emphasis on shoulder stretching. Coach says tomorrow a lighter day. Do 2 apparatus and give legs a rest. Lots of stretching, though. Continue practicing the Onodi on low beam for down the road.

6:00-6:15 pm   Complete physical therapy before leaving the gym

Notes: iced ankles while sitting in splits

6:30-6:45 pm   Drive home for dinner

6:45 pm   Dinner

7:15 pm   Shower

7:45 pm   Homework (and physical therapy), down time

10:00 pm   Lights out!

Men's Events

When men reach an elite level, they increase their training and time spent in the gym. Unlike the women, men's events include several apparatus that place a great deal of stress on the upper body and require enormous strength. The men follow a strict training plan involving strength training, stretching/flexibility, specific drills for each of their events and, of course, training of their routines to get ready for competition. Most athletes at the competitve level have 2 training sessions a day for a total of 5 to 6 hours, 5 to 6 times a week.

Curtis Hibbert
1990 Commonwealth Games Champion
Canadian 1987 World Silver Medalist in High Bar

CURTIS HIBBERT

I started gymnastics very young ... so young in fact, that Elfi was taller than I was! Initially I was more fascinated by the bleachers than the equipment. I spent most of my time climbing up and then running back down. But it didn't take me long to catch on. I started traveling for gymnastics when I was 15. To be honest, I couldn't wait. Because I came from a large family — 3 boys and 3 girls — there wasn't much privacy at home. Being on the road felt like an exciting retreat.

My greatest influence in the sport has been Ron Galimore. He was the only black gymnast I knew who had achieved greatness. He inspired me when I watched him perform on the vault at the USA National Championships. I was the only black gymnast at my gym. He made me feel comfortable about being in the sport.

BELA KAROLYI
National Team Coordinator for USA Women

I have 2 favorite moments in my career. Nadia, of course; hers was a tremendous achievement, one that had never before been accomplished. The second was Mary Lou Retton in 1984. Here was a young girl who had grown up in a different society, with a very different mentality from me — and Nadia. But both were tremendous children and athletes. They proved to me that kids are the same everywhere; they all have the same ambitions and dreams.

Gymnastics is a sport that provides incredible challenges. You'll discover a lot about yourself, your strengths and weaknesses. There are no machines involved ... just you, your mind and your body! My advice to kids just starting out is to get involved, enjoy and participate. Then, set some goals for yourself — small ones — while you're learning and getting the hang of it. Show your moves to your friends and family. Perform with pride, confidence and self-esteem! Appreciate the sport and all that it can teach you.

TIM DAGGETT

My first encounter with gymnastics was pure coincidence. I was involved in another high school sport and was heading down the hall for a drink when I peered through the gym door's window. I saw a guy swinging on a bar that was about 10 feet high in the air.

He picked up speed every time (later I'd learn he was doing "giants") and finally let go, his body flying about 13 feet high in the air, doing a back flip and then, with no effort at all, landing on 2 feet. Wow! I couldn't believe it.

So I began to compete. I never felt like I was missing out on anything — I loved the sport and for 17 years, it was my best friend. It was the first thing I thought of when I woke up and the last thing I thought about before falling asleep. It was who I was.

Tim Daggett
1984 Olympic Gold Medallist, USA
Scored a perfect 10 that clinched the Gold for the USA Men's Team on High Bar

Trade Secrets

Every athlete has 1 or 2 secrets they use to get through the pressures of competing. It might be a special food, a good-luck charm, a special outfit or a ritual the morning of a meet. Here are some stories from me and some of my friends.

Kim Zmeskal-Burdette
1991 American World Champion, 1992 Olympian, Bronze Team, USA

At first, I didn't carry a good luck charm. But once Bela Karolyi started coaching me, it became a ritual to find a lucky penny before every meet. It never seemed to fail that someone would stumble upon one. I always felt more confident once I was holding the penny.

Yvonne Tousek
Five-year Senior National Team member for Canada, Olympian in 1996, Triple Gold Medalist at 1999 Pan Am Games, four-time World Championship Team Member

I do have rituals. I'm kind of quirky that way. For luck, I take a toy Canadian Mountie bear with a flag on his stomach to every meet. I also put my handgrips for the bars on in a certain way. I wear certain clothes the day of the meet and do things in a special order for competition. Before the 1996 Olympics, people gave me cards, trinkets and stuffed animals. I brought them all to Atlanta for luck!

Curtis Hibbert
1990 Commonwealth Games Champion, Canadian 1987 World Silver Medalist in High Bar

Although I didn't have a particular good luck charm, the night before every competition I would play solitaire until I won. Sometimes I had to stay up pretty late! That was my version of luck. Being in the right place at the right time helps, but basically I believe you have to work hard and be prepared.

Elfi Schlegel with her good luck ladybugs at Schlegel's Gymnastics Centre, in Oakville, Canada.

Elfi Schlegel
1978 Canadian National Champion
1978 Commonwealth Games Gold Medalist
1979 Pam Am Games Gold and Bronze Medalist
1980 World Bronze Medalist in Vault
1980 Olympian

In 1978, my mother and younger sister accompanied me to the Commonwealth Games in Edmonton. Before the all-around finals, a ladybug landed on my leg. My mom was sure this was a good omen. Without letting on, she put the ladybug into a small jar along with some grass, poked holes in the lid and put it into her purse. That night, I won the Games. The reporters swarming around us asked my mother if she was proud. She showed them the ladybug in the jar and the reporters went crazy! They all wrote about my lucky ladybug. When we returned to Toronto it was to a mound of cards and presents, all with a ladybug theme. It's still my good luck charm.

Winning and Losing

Winning is great ... but losing never feels the same way.

However, you should look on losing as a great learning opportunity. Losing makes you a stronger athlete. It teaches you to dig down, identify what went wrong and learn how to improve your performance.

And winning isn't necessarily all it's cracked up to be. Being on top adds pressure. You're always looking over your shoulder at potential rivals and trying to find a way to stay ahead.

Winning and losing can lead to a black-and-white view of a sport. Try to focus on progress, not perfection. If you didn't give your best performance, at least you gave your best *possible* performance at that moment. Give yourself a break! Enjoying the sport of gymnastics is not about how many trophies line your mantel. It's about improving the quality of your life with a sport that you love.

YVONNE TOUSEK
Five-year Senior National Team member for Canada, 1996 Olympian, Triple Gold Medalist at 1999 Pan Am Games, four-time World Championship Team Member

I started gymnastics when I was four. I wasn't coordinated at all but I was full of energy. My first competition was a disaster. I got to the floor event, started in on my routine and forgot everything. I burst into tears and ran off. Not a great beginning. Years later, I had a similarly excruciating experience. I'd just come home from competing in Europe and I was jet-lagged. I had another competition in only a few days. Clearly I wasn't ready, because when the competition came, I fell off the beam 3 times. I was spending more time on the floor than on the beam! What a nightmare. The next day I did the same routine and nailed it. It's all about being brave enough to keep trying. I did — and I made it to the Olympics. That's the ultimate dream for any athlete. All those years of training do finally pay off.

Elfi Schlegel winning team gold at the 1979 Pan Am Games.

Elfi's Scrapbook

I remember winning my first competition. I won a trophy for my efforts, while the second- and third-place athletes won medals. I was only 7 so my parents had to help me understand why I couldn't have a medal necklace like my friends!

Springing Forward

Success is not about winning an Olympic gold medal. It's about trying, learning and making an effort to push beyond a place where once you thought of giving up.

Each of us decides what our path will be. The sport of gymnastics has made me who I am today. It has given me a career, a community and a cause. It has taught me many life lessons, such as determination, teamwork and perseverance. Those qualities are important in all aspects of life, not just sports.

I am looking forward to meeting the next child who embarks on their first recreational gymnastics lesson. That child will look at gymnastics with fresh eyes and an open heart. And with that point of view, anything is possible.

Glossary

Agility: the ability to move quickly and with ease.

Amplitude: the size of the movement (i.e. the swing on bars), the height, flight, distance or body angles displayed by a gymnast performing a skill. In general, the bigger the better.

Apparatus: the equipment used in the sport of artistic and rhythmic gymnastics. In artistic gymnastics the equipment includes the vault, bars, beam and floor. In rhythmic gymnastics the equipment includes rope, hoop, ball, clubs and ribbon.

Artistic Gymnastics: a branch of gymnastics that involves performing various skills, such as vault, uneven bars, balance beam, floor, pommel horse, still rings, vault, parallel bars and horizontal bar on an apparatus.

Choreography: the art of combining skill and dance elements to create a routine.

Code of Points: the rules that govern the sport, made by the FIG and compiled in the Code of Points book. This book includes the skills used in artistic and rhythmic gymnastics. The Code of Points is updated every 4 years to allow for the evolution of the sport.

FIG: Fédération Internationale de Gymnastique. The organizing body for international gymnastics competitions including the Olympics. FIG makes the rules, trains and certifies judges, and determines how competitions are run.

Glide kip: a basic skill that is performed on the bars (by both men and women) and is used today as a connection skill in a routine. A glide swing progression is important to know prior to attempting this skill. (A glide swing plus a pull-up to front support is the basic kip action.)

NCAA: National Collegiate Athletic Association.

NCCP: National Coaching Certification Program. A Canadian initiative designed as a standard for coaching development.

Plyometrics: a training technique used to improve explosiveness and power.

Re-grasp: the action of letting go and catching the bars with your hands.

Rhythmic gymnastics: a branch of gymnastics that involves performing various skills, such as rope, hoop, ball, ribbon and clubs with an apparatus.

Routine: a combination of movements displaying a full range of skills.

Salto: a forward, backward or sideward rotation without the use of hands.

Gymnastics Contacts and Web Sites

USA Gymnastics (USAG)
Pan American Plaza
201 South Capitol Avenue,
Suite 300
Indianapolis, IN 46225 USA
Phone: 317-237-5050
Fax: 317-237-5069
www.usa-gymnastics.org
Email:
swhitlock@usa-gymnastics.org

This is the official Web site of the United States Gymnastic Federation. It has information on the regions, states and clubs throughout the United States and offers biographies and homepages of various gymnastics athlete's from around the world. It also features an event and television broadcast calendar. It provides links to other sports in the gymnastic family and to other gymnastic-related web pages around the world, such as the Federation Internationale Gymnastique (FIG).

Fédération Internationale de
Gymnastique (FIG)
Rue des Oeuches 10,
CP 359, 2740 Moutier 1,
Switzerland
Phone: +41 32 494 64 10
Fax: +41 32 494 64 19
www.gymnastics.worldsport.com
Email:
fig.gymnastics@worldsport.org

This is the official Web site of the International Gymnastic Federation. It provides historical information, a guide to gymnastics, a glossary of terms, the rules that govern the sport, results of international events and biographies and interviews of various athletes. It also has links to other sports Web sites.

Gymnastics Canada
Gymnastiques (GCG)
1600 James Naismith Drive,
Suite 510
Gloucester, ON K1B 5N4
Phone: 613-748-5637
Fax: 613-748-5691
www.gymcan.org
Email:
gymcan@istar.ca

The Canadian Gymnastic Federation's Web site (offered in both French and English) includes information on all provincial organizations, national team athlete profiles, competition results, a calendar of upcoming gymnastics events, photo archives, press releases and links to other gymnastics Web sites around the world (including the Cirque du Soleil).

Acknowledgments

Special thanks to all those involved in making this book happen: Holly Abraham, Anita Botnen Fisher, Tim Daggett, Kirk Dunn, Marc Dunn, Loree Galimore at USAG, Susan Harris, Curtis Hibbert, Bela Karolyi, Ann-Marie Kerr, Rob Penner at NBC Sports, Luan Peszek and Chris Saunders at USAG, Janine Rankin at Gymnastics Ontario, Philippe Silacci at the FIG, Sam Silverstein and Jeff Dinski at NBCOlympics.com, Lise Simard at CGC, Betty Tate-Pineau, Andrea Schlegel, Yvonne Tousek, Kim Zmeskal-Burdette, Fiona Van Wissen and the children who appear in this book: Boulton Doolittle, Robin King, Sara Sowinski, Lauren Swant. Also, thanks to photographer Horst Herget.

Photo Credits

All photos by Horst Herget Photography, Toronto, Canada, except as follows:

Page 18 © Elfi Schlegel.
Page 33 © Elfi Schlegel.
Page 93 © The University of Florida Archives.
Page 95 © CP Picture Archives.
Page 96 © CP Picture Archives/Gravel.
Page 97 © CP Picture Archives.
Page 98 © CP Picture Archives/John Gaps III.
Page 100 © Elfi Schlegel.
Page 102 © Patrik Nichols.
Page 103 © Elfi Schlegel.
Page 106 © Kim Zmeskal-Burdette.
Page 110 © CP Picture Archives/Andrew Vaughan.
Page 112 © Tim Daggett.
Page 116 © Elfi Schlegel.
Page 120 (photo of Elfi Schlegel) © Patrik Nichols.
Page 120 (photo of Claire Ross Dunn) © Helen Tansey.

Index

About the Authors

Elfi Schlegel is one of Canada's brightest gymnastic lights. She was a member of the Canadian National Team from 1976 to 1985, won 2 gold medals at the 1978 Commonwealth Games and in 1979 won a team gold and individual bronze medal at the Pan Am Games. Elfi won Canada's only World Cup gymnastics medal, a bronze in the vault, in 1980 and was a member of the Canadian Olympic Team that honored the US boycott of the 1980 Moscow Olympic Summer Games. Elfi was also a six-time NCAA All-American while attending the University of Florida on a gymnastic scholarship. She got her start as a gymnastics commentator at the age of 17 and since then has worked for CTV and CBC. Currently she is a sports commentator for NBC. In 1998, Elfi opened Schlegel's Gymnastics Centre in Oakville, Ontario. She lives in Toronto and is married to Olympic beach volleyball player Marc Dunn.

Claire Ross Dunn, a graduate of Norman Jewison's Canadian Film Centre, is a Toronto-based writer working mostly in film and television. Currently she is working on a book for children *Esmerelda Snoot Makes Widgets*, and is developing an educational program based on Esmerelda's adventures. Claire has also worked as a film producer and actor. She is married and has a 2 year old girl named Findley.